CONTENTS

RULING REPTILES

Dinosaurs included the biggest land animals that have ever existed on Earth. They were reptiles – like today's snakes and lizards – but they were not the only ones alive during prehistoric times. They shared the world with many other giant reptiles, including ones that swam, and ones that flew on wings made of skin. By the end of the Cretaceous Period, 65 million years ago, all of them became extinct.

Cretaceous coast

Watched by pterosaurs flying overhead, a *Lambeosaurus* herd makes its way along the coast in late Cretaceous times. The long reign of the reptiles is nearing its cataclysmic end, but for the moment, reptiles still hold sway on land, in the air and in the sea. *Lambeosaurus* was a duck-billed dinosaur, or hadrosaur, and it fed on plants, tearing up mouthfuls with its beak-shaped jaws. Many other dinosaurs were carnivorous, using teeth, jaws or claws to catch their prey.

On its head, Lambeosaurus had a distinctive hollow crest.

Lambeosaurus could move on just its back legs alone, or on all fours.

A large crest counterbalanced the beak.

Pteranodon

Lambeosaurus

Like all pterosaurs, Pteranodon had an extra-long fourth finger that held open its wings.

> **REPTILE** - *an animal with scaly skin that lays eggs or gives birth to live young*

◉ FLYING GIANTS

When the dinosaurs were alive, pterosaurs criss-crossed the skies on leathery wings made of skin. Most had long jaws shaped like a beak, and some had bony, backward-pointing crests. The smallest pterosaurs were not much bigger than a crow, but the largest – called *Quetzalcoatlus* – had a wingspan of 10m, making it the largest flying animal of all time. Instead of flapping, it probably soared on outstretched wings.

Quetzalcoatlus

Using its long neck and interlocking teeth, Elasmosaurus lunged at passing fish. It belonged to a group of reptiles called plesiosaurs.

Elasmosaurus

With its streamlined body and narrow beak, Platypterygius was a typical fish-like reptile, or ichthyosaur. It gave birth to live young.

Platypterygius

❯ Dinosaurs lived on land, but it is likely that many could swim to cross rivers or to escape from floods.

EVOLUTION – *small changes that build up over generations, making living things better at survival*

DINOSAUR AGE

The Dinosaur Age lasted over 160 million years. During that time, dinosaurs evolved many different shapes for different ways of life. Some moved on all fours and fed on plants, while others ran on their back legs and hunted living prey. There were over 10 major groups of dinosaurs, but not all of them existed at the same time. Some of the earliest kinds died out long before the Dinosaur Age came to an end.

ceratosaurs

allosaurs

⊖ THE BIG SPLIT

Early on in their history, dinosaurs split into two different lines. Lizard-hipped dinosaurs, or saurischians, included all the meat-eating kinds, as well as the enormous plant-eaters called sauropods. They are shown in the main picture above in blue branches of the family tree. Bird-hipped dinosaurs, or ornithischians, were all vegetarians. They are shown in yellow in the picture above. Confusingly, the ancestors of birds were lizard-hipped.

bird-hipped

lizard-hipped

tyrannosaurs

birds

  Dinosaurs belonged to a group of reptiles called archosaurs, which also includes living reptiles and birds.

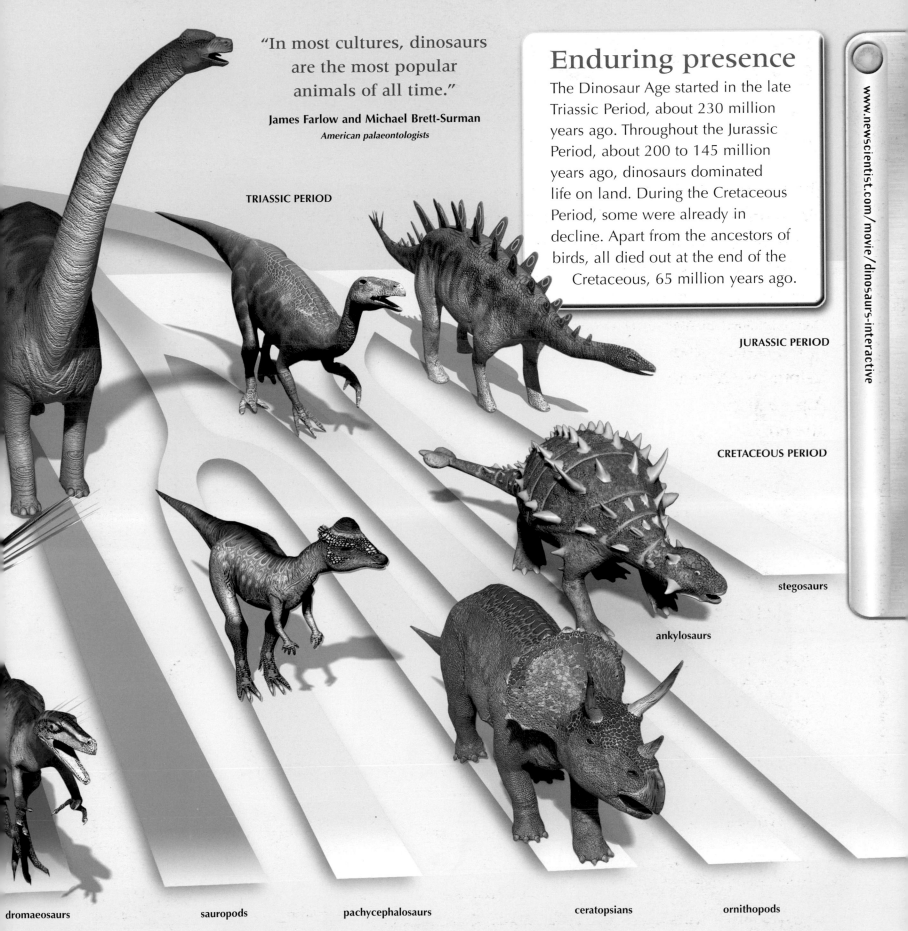

"In most cultures, dinosaurs are the most popular animals of all time."

James Farlow and Michael Brett-Surman
American palaeontologists

TRIASSIC PERIOD

Enduring presence

The Dinosaur Age started in the late Triassic Period, about 230 million years ago. Throughout the Jurassic Period, about 200 to 145 million years ago, dinosaurs dominated life on land. During the Cretaceous Period, some were already in decline. Apart from the ancestors of birds, all died out at the end of the Cretaceous, 65 million years ago.

JURASSIC PERIOD

CRETACEOUS PERIOD

stegosaurs

ankylosaurs

dromaeosaurs

sauropods

pachycephalosaurs

ceratopsians

ornithopods

DINOSAUR REMAINS

Almost everything known about dinosaurs comes from fossilized bones. Sometimes, these are found by accident, by amateur fossil hunters, but many are unearthed by scientific experts, or palaeontologists, in places that are rich in fossil-bearing rocks. In some regions, hundreds of fossils are found together. The bones are often mixed up, creating bone beds or 'dinosaur graveyards' that date back many millions of years.

Dragon bones

People found fossils long before the science of fossil-hunting began. In China, dinosaur fossils were thought to be the bones of dragons. Ground up, they were used as a medicine. Today, China is one of the world's most important fossil-hunting regions.

Giant on show

The world's tallest dinosaur fossil is a *Giraffatitan* in Berlin's Humboldt Museum. Found in Tanzania in the early 1900s, it was not displayed until 1937, because it took so long to assemble. It towers 12m high – equivalent to a 4-storey building.

HOW FOSSILS FORM

Animals fossilize when their dead remains are covered by waterborne sediment or by sand. The soft parts slowly disintegrate, but the bones gradually turn to stone. More sediment builds up above the bones, burying them deep beneath the ground. Over millions of years, the rock layers may become tilted. If the rock above wears away, the fossil is then exposed.

1. Dinosaur trapped by flood

2. Body covered by water

3. Sediment covers remains

4. Fossil slowly forms and rock layers become tilted

5. Erosion exposes fossil

  > The biggest dinosaur bone known is a shoulderblade from *Supersaurus* – it measures 2.4m high.

Wall of bones

At the Dinosaur National Monument in Utah, USA, a palaeontologist chips away rock to uncover a fossilized bone. This rock face contains over 1,500 bones, belonging to sauropods and other giant dinosaurs. The rock was originally river sediment, which covered up the dinosaurs when they died. The bones are jumbled up, probably because the remains were eaten by scavenging animals – mainly other dinosaurs.

Metal probes and soft brushes are used to expose fragile fossils without causing damage.

SMALL BEGINNINGS

The world's first dinosaurs appeared about 230 million years ago. At first, they were smaller than many other reptiles, but their descendants went on to become the most successful reptiles of all time. The oldest dinosaurs found so far come from Madagascar, but one of the best known was discovered in Argentina in 1991. Called *Eoraptor*, or 'dawn raider', it was a fast-moving, lightweight predator, only about a metre long.

slender, mobile neck

Standing tall

Sprinting on its strong back legs, *Eoraptor* carries off a lizard it has just caught. With its upright stance and small arms, *Eoraptor* was very different to other reptiles, which moved with their legs sprawled out, and their bodies close to the ground. *Eoraptor* was a primitive predatory dinosaur, or theropod. It died out about 225 million years ago, but theropods went on to include giants such as *Tyrannosaurus rex* – one of the biggest hunters that has ever walked the Earth.

flexible hands with fingers that could grasp

> Predatory dinosaurs used their teeth to grab and tear, but they could not chew.

⊖ TREASURE TROVE

Herrerasaurus skull, Valley of the Moon

Eoraptor was found in Argentina's Valley of the Moon – a desert region famous for its fossils. Another very early dinosaur, called *Herrerasaurus*, was also found here. Both dinosaurs lived about 228 million years ago, but *Herrerasaurus* was much bigger than *Eoraptor*, measuring up to 6m long. The world's oldest dinosaur fossils, from Madagascar, are about 2 million years older still. They were left by plant eaters that walked on all fours.

www.projectexploration.org/eoraptor.htm

tail used as counterbalance for head and neck

hinge-like ankle-joint let foot bend up or down

three toes made contact with the ground

"We are just a couple of steps away from the ancestor of all dinosaurs."

Paul Sereno
leader of the team that discovered Eoraptor

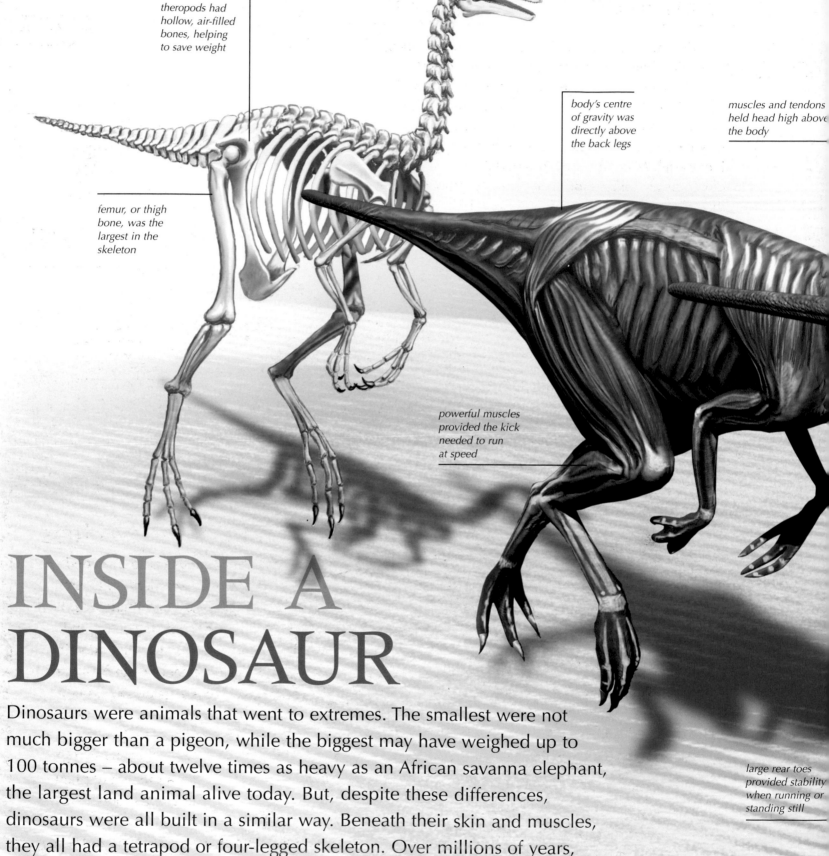

theropods had hollow, air-filled bones, helping to save weight

femur, or thigh bone, was the largest in the skeleton

body's centre of gravity was directly above the back legs

muscles and tendons held head high above the body

powerful muscles provided the kick needed to run at speed

large rear toes provided stability when running or standing still

INSIDE A DINOSAUR

Dinosaurs were animals that went to extremes. The smallest were not much bigger than a pigeon, while the biggest may have weighed up to 100 tonnes – about twelve times as heavy as an African savanna elephant, the largest land animal alive today. But, despite these differences, dinosaurs were all built in a similar way. Beneath their skin and muscles, they all had a tetrapod or four-legged skeleton. Over millions of years, the skeleton's proportions changed to suit many different ways of life.

 > *Gallimimus* belonged to a group of theropods called ornithomimids, or 'bird mimics'.

⊜ MIDGETS AND MONSTERS

The smallest dinosaur found so far is *Microraptor*, a tiny feathered theropod just 40cm long. At the other extreme, the biggest dinosaurs known include *Argentinosaurus* and *Supersaurus*, both of which grew up to 40m long. *Argentinosaurus* may have tipped the scales at 100 tonnes, making it outweigh *Microraptor* by 200,000 times. Although dinosaurs are famous for their huge proportions, they also included a large number of middle-sized animals, such as *Coelophysis*. It was built for speed and agility, rather than power.

Microraptor – 40cm

Argentinosaurus – 40m

Coelophysis – 3m

sideways-pointing eyes gave a wide view of surroundings

hard-edged beak without teeth

body skin may have been scaly or covered with short feathers

Gallimimus

scaly skin on legs

hands may have been used for digging up food

Life on two legs

Gallimimus was a theropod dinosaur, standing up to 4m high. Like other theropods, it moved on its back legs, and had small arms that ended in three-fingered hands. It had an elongated skull, with beak-like jaws. Instead of living by hunting alone, it probably fed on a mixture of plant and animal food.

COLOUR AND DISGUISE

A huge amount is known about dinosaur skeletons, but no one knows what dinosaur bodies would have looked like from the outside. Traditionally, they are often painted a plain grey, like gigantic rhinos or elephants. However, small dinosaurs – such as *Coelophysis* – may well have been brightly coloured, like many lizards are today. Bold patterns would have broken up their outline, helping them to blend in with their background as they stalked their prey.

Coelophysis **may have had brightly coloured, patterned skin that camouflaged them amongst the shadows of the undergrowth.**

⊖ SOFT TOUCH

Living reptiles are all covered with scales. Although dinosaurs were reptiles, fossils of some species – such as *Sinosauropteryx* – show that they were covered with fine, fuzzy down. Others had simple feathers, even though they could not fly. These body coverings might have been brightly coloured, helping dinosaurs to attract partners when the time came to mate.

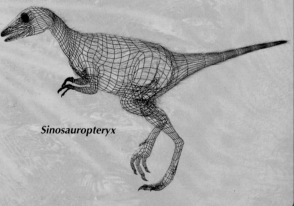

Sinosauropteryx

> Dinosaur colours were produced by chemical pigments, such as melanin, stored inside cells in their skin.

Out of the shadows

This group of *Coelophysis* is feeding on a kill. Their markings look eye-catching in the open, but they would have worked as camouflage in sun-dappled shade. *Coelophysis* may have had different markings in males and females, and another set of markings that helped adults to identify their young. These juvenile markings would have changed when the young became ready to breed. Some dinosaurs may also have changed colour to express their mood – a trick used by chameleons and other modern lizards.

http://news.bbc.co.uk/1/hi/7124969.stm

Mummified skin

When dinosaurs died, their soft body parts usually rotted before they became fossilized. But sometimes, a dinosaur's body would dry out, forming a mummified corpse. One of these 'dinomummies' shows the knobbly pattern of a hadrosaur's skin in an amazing amount of detail for something over 65 million years old.

nostrils may have
been high on
head, or closer
to the snout

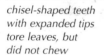

chisel-shaped teeth
with expanded tips
tore leaves, but
did not chew

Brachiosaurus

GIANT PLANT EATERS

Plant-eating dinosaurs called sauropods were the largest animals
ever to have walked the Earth. The longest measured up to 40m
from head to tail, and may have weighed more than 100 tonnes.
Typical sauropods probably held their necks and tails horizontally,
or at a slight slope, but brachiosaurs were specially built to reach
upwards into trees. When fully grown, they could reach twice
as high as a giraffe. With their heads in the treetops, they used
their teeth like a rake to tear off mouthfuls of leaves.

 > Sauropod fossils and footprints have been found on every continent except Antarctica.

araucaria leaves were hard, and often ended in sharp points

Head for heights

In this scene from the late Jurassic Period, about 160 million years ago, a herd of brachiosaurs are feeding on araucaria trees. Unlike other sauropods, brachiosaurs had extra-large front legs, which contributed to their 12m height. Palaeontologists once believed that brachiosaurs waded deep into water, because fossils seem to show that their nostrils were high on their heads. This is now thought unlikely, because the water pressure would have stopped their lungs working.

The large front legs gave brachiosaurs high shoulders and a sloping back.

Stomach stones

Instead of chewing, many dinosaurs swallowed stones to help them digest food. The stones, called gastroliths, lodged in a dinosaur's stomach, where they ground up the food after it had been swallowed. These gastroliths were found near a sauropod's ribcage in New Mexico. They have been worn smooth through use.

⊖ DINOSAUR DROPPINGS

Large dinosaurs had to eat an enormous amount of food to keep themselves alive. Their droppings were equally impressive, and they sometimes fossilized. Fossils like these, known as coprolites, can be over 60cm long. Looked at under a microscope, a coprolite often reveals ancient fragments of plants or bone, giving some idea of the kind of dinosaur that left it behind.

fossilized dinosaur droppings probably made by a sauropod called *Titanosaurus*

mature adults formed a barrier between the predators and the herd's young

Deinonychus

Deinonychus *was far smaller than Iguanodon, but had a sabre-like claw on each hind foot*

Iguanodon

LIFE IN A HERD

Despite their size, plant-eating dinosaurs lived in a world full of danger, where predators could attack at any time. To protect themselves, many herbivores lived in herds. They fed and travelled together, and raised their young in the safety of a group. By keeping close to one another, they made it harder for predators to single out one from the crowd. However, life in a herd could sometimes be dangerous. Occasionally, whole herds died when disasters suddenly wiped them out.

at speed, Iguanodon *moved on its back feet, with its front legs off the ground*

 > *Iguanodon* was named after its teeth, which look like large versions of an iguana's (a plant-eating lizard).

⊖ DEADLY TRAP

Iguanodon was discovered in 1822, making it one of the first dinosaurs to be studied by scientists. At first, its thumb spike caused confusion – an early drawing showed the spike on *Iguanodon*'s nose! This mistake was later corrected. In 1878, coal miners at Bernissart, Belgium, discovered an entire herd of *Iguanodon* buried underground. The dinosaurs had fallen into a ravine, and were slowly fossilized inside seams of coal.

drawing showing thumb spike on *Iguanodon*'s nose

Closing ranks

In early Cretaceous Period forests, a herd of *Iguanodon* senses trouble in the air. The dinosaurs are being pursued by a pack of *Deinonychus*, and they are preparing for a possible attack. The adults have positioned themselves around their vulnerable young, and are doing their best to stage an orderly retreat. If the attack comes, the adult *Iguanodon* will fight back, using the lethal spikes that they have on their thumbs.

thumb was armed with a long, sharply pointed spike

http://www.dinohunters.com/iguanodon/bernissart.htm

DINOSAUR TRACKS

When scientists first studied dinosaur tracks, they thought they belonged to giant flightless birds. Since then, these fascinating 'trace fossils' have been identified and found all over the world. Their shape and spacing can show what kind of dinosaurs left them, and even what they were doing at the time. Dinosaurs were creatures of habit. Fossilized trackways, or 'dino highways', suggest that they used some routes for thousands of years.

> TRACE FOSSIL – preserved remains that show how animals lived

Apatosaurus had a stride length of up to 5m, and it moved its legs in diagonal pairs when walking.

Sauropod prints are deep and round. The rear feet left claw marks, but the front ones often did not.

Vertical tracks

Just like fossilized bones, fossilized tracks often change position after they have formed. The tracks shown here, in northern Argentina, were left by a theropod striding across an ancient shoreline. Over millions of years, earth movements slowly tipped them up on edge. A geologist standing beneath them shows their scale.

Gallimimus could probably run at over 50km/h in short bursts.

Gallimimus and other theropods (meat eaters) left three-toed prints.

"...footprints are those of creatures in the full tide of life."

Richard Swann Lull (1867–1957)
American palaeontologist and track expert

Traces in time

Walking across the bed of a desert lake, three different dinosaurs leave distinctive tracks in the rapidly drying mud. Like all sauropods, *Apatosaurus* had soles shaped like giant pancakes, leaving rounded tracks, often with little sign of any claws. *Gallimimus* and *Dryosaurus* left three-toed prints, like the first dinosaur tracks to be found. The faster they ran, the deeper their toes dug into the mud.

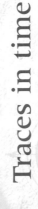

Unusually for a plant eater, *Dryosaurus* had short hands, and ran on its back legs.

At speed Dryosaurus's three-toed prints were spaced well apart.

● FOSSILIZATION

To fossilize, tracks first have to harden by drying in the sun. Next, they are gently flooded with water, which buries them in layers of sediment. As the sediment builds up, increasing pressure slowly turns it into rock. After millions of years, the rock is exposed to the air, and it begins to erode. Finally, the fossil tracks appear at the surface. With luck, the tracks are spotted before they eventually crumble away.

1. Footprint makes an impression in mud

2. Footprint fills up with more mud

3. Over millions of years, the mud turns to rock

4. Material filling the impression washes out, leaving a fossilized track

> In 2009, fossil hunters in France found sauropod tracks almost 2m across – the biggest ever discovered.

HADROSAUR – a plant-eating dinosaur with a beak-like snout, and often a crest

Whipcrack!

Diplodocus had nearly 80 vertebrae in its tail, which had a very long, slender tip. It may have been able to crack it like a whip, breaking the speed of sound. The cracking sound would have warned away predators, and may have helped *Diplodocus* to stay in touch with its own kind.

Trumpeting crest

Parasaurolophus had the largest crest of any hadrosaur, measuring up to 1.8m long. Using X-ray scanners, scientists have found that it contained hollow tubes linking the dinosaur's nostrils with the back of its throat. When *Parasaurolophus* breathed through its crest, these long tubes may have made the air reverberate, producing loud bellowing or trumpeting sounds.

crest formed by enlarged upper jaw and nasal bones

incoming air entered the crest from the nostrils

CALL OF THE WILD

Today's reptiles are mostly silent, apart from sounds they make when they move. But over 65 million years ago, the world's landscapes may have echoed with the eerie noises of hadrosaurs, or duck-billed dinosaurs. Many hadrosaurs had large crests on the tops of their heads. Some of these crests were hollow, turning them into echo chambers that might have worked like enormous trombones.

"It's the kind of sound that would easily be heard by other animals through a thick rain forest."

Tom Williamson
palaeontologist, describing a computer-generated reconstruction of Parasaurolophus*'s call*

 > Hadrosaurs have been nicknamed the 'cows of the Cretaceous', because they formed huge plant-eating herds.

air reverberated as it travelled through the crest, which may have created loud, trumpeting sounds

tubes doubled back at the tip of the crest

air flowed out of the crest to the lungs

crest contained several tube-like channels, linked to other internal spaces

http://edition.cnn.com/TECH/9712/05/dino.speaks/

⊖ FAMILY CRESTS

Edmontosaurus had a long, low skull – a shape shared by *Maiasaura* and several other hadrosaurs, but many of the hadrosaur family had conspicuous crests. *Lambeosaurus* had a crest shaped like a hatchet, with an upward-pointing blade, while *Corythosaurus* had one that looked like a helmet, flattened on either side. Hadrosaurs fed on plants. They tore off mouthfuls of food with their 'beaks', and then chewed them with a battery of teeth at the back of their jaws.

Edmontosaurus   **Lambeosaurus**   **Corythosaurus**

NERVOUS SYSTEM – *a body system that works like wiring, letting animals sense their surroundings and move*

BRAINS AND SENSES

For their size, dinosaurs often had tiny brains. But this did not mean they were stupid, because keen senses helped them to survive. Plant eaters used sight and smell to find their food. While they were feeding, their eyes and ears alerted them if anything dangerous was nearby. Fast-moving hunters such as *Troodon* had relatively large brains, and found their food mainly by sight. They were experts at spotting movement, but probably not so good at noticing prey that stood still.

Crunch!

Pachycephalosaurs had dome-shaped brain cases up to 20cm thick. At one time, scientists thought that the males used them in head-butting contests during the breeding season. However, pachycephalosaurs did not have reinforced necks, so it is more likely that they swung their heads into each other's sides, like male giraffes do today.

⊖ BRAIN POWER

Compared to their bodies, stegosaurs had the smallest brains of all dinosaurs, measuring only a few millionths of the total body weight. Stegosaurs had an extra 'mini brain', or ganglion, above their hips, to control their back legs and tail. Theropods were more intelligent, although the biggest still had minuscule brains for their size. *Troodon* and its relatives were probably top of the class in dinosaur intelligence, because their brains were well developed, and their bodies relatively small.

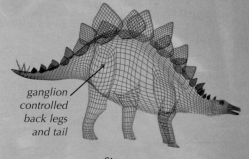

ganglion controlled back legs and tail

Stegosaurus

> *Stegosaurus*'s brain weighed about 75g – about the same as a large chicken's egg.

fluid-filled semicircular canals sensed movement, and created the sense of balance

slit-shaped pupils would have helped Troodon to spot horizontal movement in bright daylight; at night, they would have opened wide

nostrils carried air over sensory cells above the roof of the mouth, and were able to open and close

olfactory lobes at front of brain managed the sense of smell

ear opened through a simple hole in the skull

www.geo.arizona.edu/~rwright/abs2002.html

Quick-witted hunter

Troodon was only about 2m long, but it belonged to a group of advanced theropods that had unusually well-developed brains. It was probably warm-blooded, which would have enabled the whole of its nervous system to work at high speed. The shape of its brain case shows that it had a fairly good sense of smell, but its most important sense was sight. Because its eyes were so large, some experts think that it may have hunted at night.

like most dinosaurs, Troodon *may have had a poor sense of taste*

EGG MOUNTAIN

Dinosaurs bred by laying eggs, like most reptiles do today. Some of their eggs were not much larger than a chicken's, but the biggest – belonging to sauropods – were over 40cm long. At Egg Mountain, in the US state of Montana, an entire herd of duck-billed dinosaurs nested together. Fossils show that the parent dinosaurs took care of their eggs, and also collected food for the newly hatched young.

Family group

Alerted by their cheeping, a female *Maiasaura* tends her eggs and young. These dinosaurs made bowl-shaped nests and lined them with plants, which helped to keep the eggs warm. Fossils show that the young were poorly developed when they hatched – a sign that they were fed by their parents.

females nested at the same time, making it harder for predators to reach the eggs or young

⊖ LONG DROP

Small and medium-sized dinosaurs could squat to lay their eggs, but giant sauropods – such as *Apatosaurus* – could hardly bend their back legs. Their eggs faced a daunting drop of 2m or more before they hit the ground. To stop them breaking, female sauropods may have had a fleshy egg-laying tube, or ovipositor. Because the tube was soft it would not have fossilized, so none has ever been found.

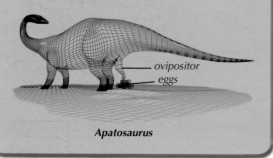

ovipositor
eggs

Apatosaurus

Nesting styles

This fossilized nest from China was constructed by a predatory theropod, towards the end of the Dinosaur Age. It contains 22 elongated eggs, arranged in a circle. Many of the eggs have broken shells, revealing tiny dinosaur skeletons inside. Not all dinosaurs were this neat – sauropods laid their eggs in rather untidy piles.

plants created heat as they rotted, incubating the eggs

 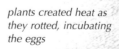 > For their size, the biggest dinosaurs laid small eggs, equivalent to a tiny fraction of their own weight.

INCUBATE – *to keep an egg warm so that the embryo inside can develop*

nests were neatly
spaced out in the
breeding colony

nest made from
earth scraped
into a ring

eggs laid
in a circle

young probably
remained in the nest
for several weeks

mature embryo
curled up inside egg

PACK ATTACK

Plant-eating dinosaurs weren't the only ones that often lived in groups. Some fast, quick-witted killers worked like wolves in a pack, singling out prey many times their own size. One of these was *Deinonychus* – a predator that used extra-large hind claws to attack its victims. Measuring about 3m long, *Deinonychus* was light enough to leap aboard its prey. Here, it set to work with its claws, bringing much bigger dinosaurs crashing to the ground.

Winning formula

Small pack-hunting killers lived throughout the Dinosaur Age. One of the earliest was *Coelophysis*. At Ghost Ranch, in New Mexico, thousands of *Coelophysis* fossils have been found together. The fossils come in two sizes – scientists think that the larger ones are males.

One against many

In a forest clearing, about 100 million years ago, a plant-eating *Tenontosaurus* is fighting for its life as a pack of *Deinonychus* slash at it with their claws. Unlike early dinosaurs, *Deinonychus* was probably warm-blooded. A covering of feathers would have kept in its body heat, enabling it to stay active even in cold conditions. Warm-blooded animals make effective hunters, but they need more fuel than cold-blooded ones to keep their bodies working. As a result, the *Deinonychus* pack would be constantly on the hunt.

Deinonychus

hands had three fingers, tipped with long claws

> *Deinonychus*'s sickle-shaped rear claws were about 12cm long.

second toe swivelled
downwards when
Deinonychus *attacked*

Tenontosaurus

extra-large claw on second
toe stayed off the ground
when Deinonychus *was on
the move, keeping it sharp*

huge rear leg muscles braced
Tyrannosaurus rex while it fed

skin may have
had scattered
feathers

Tower of strength

With teeth measuring up to 30cm long,
Tyrannosaurus rex had a 'bite-and-tear'
feeding technique that made short work
of fallen flesh. Unlike many predatory
dinosaurs, its upper jaw ended in a blunt,
U-shaped snout. This enabled it to tear
off up to 75kg of food at one go – about
the same weight as an average man.
It towered over its food on its colossal
back legs, while its tiny front legs hung
in the air. For a dinosaur, its sense of
smell was unusually good, helping
it to track down dead food.

large openings between
skull bones helped to
reduce weight of head

> SCAVENGER - *an animal that feeds mainly or entirely on dead remains*

DEATH ON TWO LEGS

Tyrannosaurus rex is the world's most famous predator, even through it vanished over 65 million years ago. We know exactly what it looked like thanks to some incredible fossil finds. One of them, nicknamed 'Sue', is amazingly well preserved – a sign that it was covered by mud or sand just after it died. But *Tyrannosaurus rex's* lifestyle remains a puzzle. Instead of being a serial killer, it may have got some or all of its food by scavenging from dead remains.

● KILLERS COMPARED

Tyrannosaurus rex weighed up to 7 tonnes, and measured up to 13m from head to tail. Despite this, it was probably not the largest land predator of all time. *Carcharodontosaurus* may have weighed over 10 tonnes, while *Giganotosaurus* tipped the scales at over 12 tonnes. The longest of all may have been *Spinosaurus* – a sail-backed hunter with jaws like a crocodile, which is thought to have fed on fish. It may have been up to 18m long.

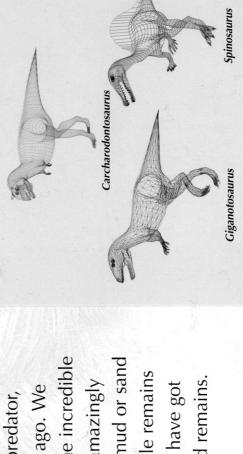

Spinosaurus

Carcharodontosaurus

Giganotosaurus

teeth at front of jaw had a backward curve and a D-shaped cross section

❯ In 2009, palaeontologists identified a miniature tyrannosaur, called *Raptorex*. It weighed only a hundredth as much as *Tyrannosaurus rex*.

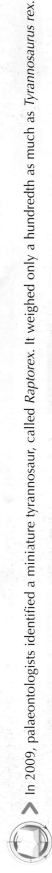

FIGHTING BACK

For plant-eating dinosaurs, survival meant being permanently on guard. If they were attacked, very few could use their teeth as weapons. Instead, some hit back by rearing up on their back legs, or by stabbing their opponents with sharp claws. *Ankylosaurus* had some of the best protection of all. The dinosaur was covered in armour plating, and its stiff tail ended in a massive club that could smash an enemy's skull.

Deadly spikes

Stegosaurus had bony plates on its back, but its real weapons were vicious spikes on its sides and at the tip of its tail. The spikes pointed outwards, so they stabbed into an enemy as *Stegosaurus* swung around.

tail spikes

Killer blow

With its 5-tonne body and superb defences, *Ankylosaurus* was built to stand and fight rather than to run away. Here, the dinosaur is fending off an *Albertosaurus* that has unwisely closed in to attack. *Ankylosaurus*'s skin was reinforced and protected with bony plates, or osteoderms, and its tail club could swing with shattering force if anything came too close. Its only weak point was its underside, which had unarmoured skin.

bony plates protected each eye

Ankylosaurus

⊖ REARING UP

Sauropods had legs like pillars, and spent almost all of their time on all fours. However, faced with danger, some could rear up on their back legs in a bid to trample an attacker. Many kinds, including *Barosaurus*, had a large claw on the inside of each front foot, which could have ripped downwards into an attacker. However, rearing up could put the huge animal off-balance, sending it crashing to the ground.

***Barosaurus* rearing up**

> Ankylosaur body armour was so strong that if these dinosaurs were around today, they would be bulletproof.

tail club had two large
lobes and weighed
over 50kg

Albertosaurus

...n is protected
...bony plates
...d knobs, or
...eoderms

rows of extra-large
plates ran along
back and sides

Scissorhands

Therizinosaurus had the longest
claws ever known – they could
be nearly 1m long. They might
have worked as weapons, but
their main job was probably
gathering plant food.

MORTAL COMBAT

In 1971, fossil hunters in Mongolia made the find of the century: two dinosaurs locked in combat. One of them was *Velociraptor*, a fast-moving predator. The other was *Protoceratops* – a 1.5m-long plant eater with jaws like a beak. The two animals were evenly matched, but something brought the fight to a sudden end. The most likely explanation is that a collapsing cliff smothered them in sand. Over 75 million years later, the fossil fighters are still locked together in their deadly embrace.

"...collapsing in death, the two bodies were covered by blowing sand before scavengers could find the bodies and tear them apart."

David Spalding
geologist based in Canada

Protoceratops was one of the first ceratopsians – a group of dinosaurs that evolved spectacular frills and enormous horns.

1. *Protoceratops stands its ground as Velociraptor approaches – perhaps because it was guarding its nest and eggs.*

2. *Protoceratops lunges forwards to defend itself, while Velociraptor tries to lash out with the killer claws on its back feet.*

Robber cousins

Velociraptor was discovered in 1922, during a US expedition to Mongolia. Its name means 'fast robber', showing that it was very quick on its feet. Velociraptor was closely related to Deinonychus and may also have been warm-blooded.

> FRILL – *a shield-like extension of the skull that sweeps backwards, protecting the neck*

FLAMING CLIFFS

The fighting dinosaurs were found in a part of the Gobi desert called the Flaming Cliffs. This remote desert landscape is where *Protoceratops* was discovered in 1922. A year later, another expedition made a find almost as famous as the fighting dinosaurs – an adult *Oviraptor* sitting on its eggs.

one of the world's great fossil-hunting regions

3. With one of its front legs trapped by *Protoceratops's* beak, *Velociraptor* falls on its side, kicking at its enemy's neck and underside.

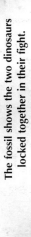

The fossil shows the two dinosaurs locked together in their fight.

Fatal encounter

Compared to *Velociraptor*, *Protoceratops* was slow-moving, which made it an easy target. However, its skull was armoured with a protective frill, and it could inflict bone-crushing injuries with its bite. *Velociraptor* was equipped with a lethal claw on each foot, but in this fight they may have led to its downfall. One of them became caught in *Protoceratops's* neck, ensuring that *Velociraptor* was also buried by sand.

❯ *Velociraptor* may have had a covering of feathers, like many other small theropod dinosaurs.

SAVING WEIGHT

Ceratopsians' head shields, or frills, could be twice the size of a car door. *Triceratops*'s frill was made of solid bone, which meant that it was extremely heavy. Many of its relatives saved weight by having frills with large gaps in the bone, which were covered by skin. *Styracosaurus* had two gaps, and its frill was edged with horns and spikes. Even so, the animal still weighed 3 tonnes.

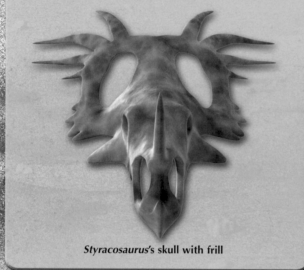

Styracosaurus's skull with frill

older teeth were continually replaced by new ones underneath

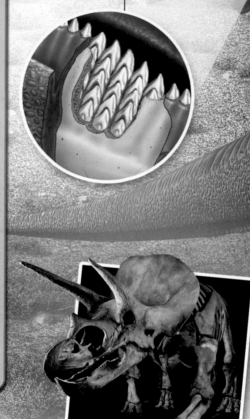

RHINO DINOSAURS

With its three horns and its gigantic head shield or frill, *Triceratops* was one of the most distinctive plant eaters from the end of the Dinosaur Age. It weighed up to 6 tonnes, and its skull was one of the biggest ever grown by a land animal, with a maximum length of over 2.5m. Like other ceratopsians, or 'rhino dinos', it used its horns against predators, but males probably turned them against their rivals when the time came to breed.

Giant head

This fossilized skeleton, found in Alberta, Canada, shows the huge proportions of *Triceratops*'s skull. The skull measured about a third of its total body length. It had three horns, up to 1m long, and jaws that ended in a beak. The beak was covered by a layer of horn, just like a bird's.

 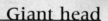 Ceratopsians may have been able to signal to each other by 'blushing' the skin covering their frills.

Locking horns

Straining with all their might, two male *Triceratops* struggle for supremacy during the breeding season. In contests like these, rival males would probably have rammed or bulldozed their opponents, rather than trying to inflict injuries with their horns. However, these ritual battles could take a vicious turn: some fossil skulls show serious gouges where horns hit home.

FISHING DINOSAURS

Dinosaurs were land animals, and almost all the carnivorous kinds hunted land-dwelling prey. *Baryonyx* was different. Although it was a land-dwelling predator, it lurked by the sides of rivers and lakes, ready to seize fish that swam within range. As soon as a fish was close enough, it would plunge its jaws beneath the surface, or hook it with its front claws. Within seconds, the wriggling fish would be hauled onto land, often to be swallowed whole.

Sudden death

Baryonyx had jaws like a crocodile's, with nearly 100 conical, sharply pointed teeth set in a narrow snout that widened towards the tip. It caught small fish with its teeth alone, but for bigger fish it used its claws. Measuring over 30cm long, the claws stabbed fish and then swept them out of the water and onto dry land. Fossilized fish scales have been found with its remains, along with bones from smaller dinosaurs.

bulbous snout is typical of fish-eating reptiles, including living crocodiles and gharials

> **SPINOSAUR** – a predatory dinosaur with narrow jaws and simple, conical teeth

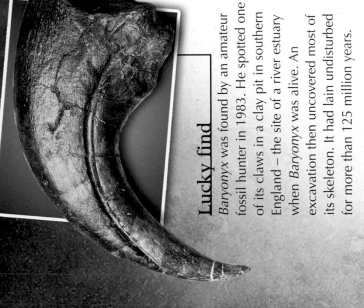

Lucky find

Baryonyx was found by an amateur fossil hunter in 1983. He spotted one of its claws in a clay pit in southern England – the site of a river estuary when *Baryonyx* was alive. An excavation then uncovered most of its skeleton. It had lain undisturbed for more than 125 million years.

catfish often live in shallow, slow-moving water, making them easy prey

teeth had a simple shape but extremely deep roots, with up to half their total length buried in the jaw

● SAIL-BACKED DINOSAURS

Baryonyx belonged to a group of hunters with highly specialized jaws. Its best-known relative is *Spinosaurus* – a colossal predator up to 18m long. Unlike *Baryonyx*, *Spinosaurus* had a giant sail along its back, held up by a row of bony spines. The tallest spines, halfway down its back, were higher than an adult man. *Spinosaurus* may have used its sail to soak up warmth from sunshine, or in breeding season displays.

Spinosaurus

> *Baryonyx* was about 9m long. Another fish-eating spinosaur, called *Suchomimus*, measured up to 12m.

Early bird

The world's oldest fossil of a true bird was found in Germany, in 1861. Called *Archaeopteryx*, it had teeth, clawed wings, and a long, bony tail. It looked like a small theropod dinosaur, but it had feathers and could fly. *Archaeopteryx* lived about 150 million years ago – earlier than many dino-birds.

outstretched arms worked as stabilizers, and helped to sweep insects towards Caudipteryx's jaws

DINO-BIRDS

In the last 20 years, scientists have made some amazing discoveries in the quarries of northeast China. As well as ancient plants and mammals, they have found fossils of feathered dinosaurs. The earliest kinds had short and simple feathers, which worked like a coat of fur. But over millions of years, their feathers became stronger, and more like the flight feathers that birds have today. Eventually, dino-birds evolved working wings, and true birds were born.

> Fossils of dino-birds are often found in ancient volcanic ash, which preserves the outline of feathers.

⊖ FOUR-WINGED FLIERS

No one knows how dino-birds started to fly. They may have begun by gliding onto their prey from trees, or they may have jumped up from the ground. Wings could also be useful when running up slopes, which is how some ground-dwelling birds use them today. Most dino-birds used their arms as wings, but some kinds – such as *Microraptor* – also had long feathers on their legs, and may have flown on all fours. These four-winged fliers eventually died out, leaving two-winged species that evolved into birds.

Microraptor

tail had a large fan of feathers at the tip

Caudipteryx

bird-like beak had a small number of simple teeth in the upper jaw

www.nhm.ac.uk/nature-online/life/dinosaurs-other-extinct-creatures/dino-birds/

High-speed chase

Swerving after a dragonfly, *Caudipteryx* stretches out its feathered arms as it closes in on its prey. It could not fly, but its feathered arms and tail helped it to steer. Its body was covered with an insulating layer of short down feathers. These would have kept its body at a warm and steady temperature – a feature shared by all birds alive today. Fossils of *Caudipteryx* were discovered in the late 1990s. They date back to the early Cretaceous Period, about 125 million years ago.

Undersea evidence

In the late 1970s, oil prospectors found a huge depression on the seabed off the coast of Mexico. Known as the Chicxulub crater, it is probably the place where the meteorite struck the Earth, ending the Dinosaur Age. The crater is nearly 200km across.

As well as dinosaurs, the great extinction swept away flying reptiles, or pterosaurs, and many of the reptiles that lived in the seas.

FATAL IMPACT

Throughout the Dinosaur Age, new kinds of dinosaurs slowly evolved, and old ones gradually became extinct. But 65 million years ago, something catastrophic happened. All the dinosaurs vanished, together with many other kinds of animal life. This worldwide disaster came from outer space, when an enormous meteorite collided with the Earth. The meteorite was destroyed during the impact, releasing as much energy as a billion atomic bombs.

Living dinosaurs

Most people would not muddle up a bird with a dinosaur, but beneath their feathers, birds are dinosaurs in disguise. Scientists even classify them as dinosaurs, because they are direct descendants of dino-birds.

Alamosaurus

World on fire

Within hours of the meteorite impact, a deadly combination of shock waves and heat swept the Earth. Blasted high into the atmosphere, billions of tonnes of dust encircled the planet, killing plant life by blocking the sunshine. Without food, plant-eating dinosaurs soon died, and large predators followed. The animal world would never be the same again.

 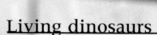 The meteorite that ended the Dinosaur Age was probably travelling at more than 70,000km/h.

"...suddenly you're dealing with an animal that isn't extinct any more. The dinosaurs are still alive."

Philip J. Currie
Canadian palaeontologist and expert on the origin of birds

arge dinosaurs were particularly ulnerable to disasters, because hey could not take cover nd needed enormous mounts of food.

Triceratops

Tyrannosaurus rex

⊖ SURVIVORS

The meteorite impact ended the Cretaceous Period, and brought the reign of the reptiles to a close. But amid the devastation, birds, mammals and some reptiles managed to survive. The biggest surviving reptiles were crocodiles, which managed to live by scavenging food from dead remains. Reptile survivors also included the ancestors of today's snakes and lizards, as well as tuataras, which belong to a group of reptiles as old as the earliest dinosaurs.

tortoise

tuatara

cobra

crocodile

http://paleobiology.si.edu/blastPast/index.html

GLOSSARY

asymmetrical
Having a lopsided shape.
Asymmetrical flight feathers are
a key feature of birds, separating
them from feathered dinosaurs.

camouflage
Shapes and colours that help an
animal to blend in with its background,
so that it can hide from its enemies
or get close to its prey.

carnivorous
Eating animals as food.

ceratopsian
A plant-eating dinosaur with a body
like a rhino, horns, and a bony head
shield or frill.

cold-blooded
An animal whose body temperature
goes up and down in step with the
temperature outside. Living reptiles are
all cold-blooded, but some dinosaurs
may have been warm-blooded instead.

crater
A circular hollow, created by a
volcanic eruption or by a meteorite
hitting the Earth.

down
A layer of short, fluffy feathers
that feathered dinosaurs used
to keep warm.

erode
To gradually wear away. Rocks are
eroded mainly by wind and rain, and
also by frost splitting them apart.

evolution
Slow changes that make living things
better at survival. Evolution happens
over many generations, instead of
during a single lifetime. It gradually
alters the way animals look, and lets
them develop new ways of life.

evolve
To change through evolution.

excavation
A careful dig designed to reveal
fossils buried in the ground.

extinct
No longer living anywhere on Earth.
Extinction can happen gradually, or
in bursts that wipe out many forms
of life at the same time.

flight feather
A long feather with a lopsided shape.
Flight feathers keep birds airborne
when they beat their wings.

fossil
Remains of living things that have
been preserved in the ground. In
most fossils, the original remains
are replaced by hard minerals,
which can keep their shape for
millions of years.

hadrosaur
A plant-eating dinosaur with
a duck-like beak, and often
a bony crest on its skull.

herbivore
Any animal that eats plants.

incubate
Keep eggs warm by sitting
on them. Birds incubate their
eggs, and so did small,
warm-blooded dinosaurs.

insulating
Slowing down heat loss, so that
something stays warm.

ift
A natural resistance to the pull of
gravity, which keeps a flying animal
in the air.

mammal
An animal that has fur, and that feeds its
young on milk. Unlike reptiles, almost
all mammals give birth to live young.

meteorite
A rock from space that penetrates the
atmosphere and hits Earth's surface.

palaeontologist
A scientist who studies prehistoric
life, using fossils and other kinds
of evidence.

pigments
Coloured chemicals that are found
in rocks and in living things.

prehistoric
Something that existed before
recorded history began.

preservation
In nature, anything that makes dead
remains keep their shape.

prey
Animals that are hunted by others as
food. Plant-eating dinosaurs were prey
animals, but so were many predatory
dinosaurs, because they were hunted
by dinosaurs larger than themselves.

pterosaur
A reptile that flew on wings made of
skin. Pterosaurs were not dinosaurs,
but they lived alongside them.

reptile
An animal with scaly skin that lays
eggs or gives birth to live young.
Reptiles include snakes, lizards,
tortoises and crocodiles, as well
as dinosaurs.

sauropod
A plant-eating dinosaur with a huge
body, and a very long neck and
tail. Sauropods included the largest
land animals that have ever lived.

scavenger
An animal that feeds on dead remains.

sediment
Small particles of mud or grit that
settle out of water.

semicircular canal
A fluid-filled space inside an animal's
head, which detects movement and
the pull of gravity.

species
A group of living things that look like
each other, and that breed only with
their own kind.

spinosaur
A type of predatory dinosaur with
narrow jaws, like a crocodile's, and
sometimes a bony crest running
down its back.

theropod
A dinosaur with small arms and
hollow bones, which walked upright
on its back legs. Most theropods were
predators, although some fed on a
mix of plant and animal food.

vertebra (pl. vertebrae)
An individual bone in the spinal
column (or backbone) of an animal.

warm-blooded
An animal that stays warm even when
the temperature outside is cold.

INDEX

INVESTIGATE

The skull of a *Tarbosaurus* from the Gobi desert – one of hundreds of dinosaur exhibits at London's Natural History Museum.

Find out more about dinosaurs and prehistoric life by visiting museums and fossil-hunting sites, or by watching and reading about these awe-inspiring animals in documentaries, films and reference books.

Museums and exhibitions

Most of the world's greatest dinosaur fossils are displayed in museums, giving you a chance to come face to face with these giants from the past.

A fossil ammonite from southern England's Jurassic coast, where crumbling rock exposes new fossils every year.

 Dinosaurs by Dougal Dixon (Natural History Museum)

 Natural History Museum, Cromwell Road, London, SW7 5BD, UK

 www.nhm.ac.uk/kids-only/dinosaurs/ and www.dinosaurisle.com

Fossil-hunting sites

Try fossil hunting at rocky places inland or on the shore. Head for areas that have sedimentary (layered) rocks. If you are on the coast, stay away from cliffs and keep a check on the tide.

 KFK Rocks and Fossils by Margaret Hynes (Kingfisher)

 Jurassic Coast, Dorset – classed as a World Heritage Site, this is one of Britain's richest fossil-hunting regions

 www.discoveringfossils.co.uk/locations.htm

Animation brings the past to life in this stunning model of *Torosaurus*, a horned dinosaur, built to appear in films.

Documentaries and movies

Chinese palaeontologist Xu Xing carefully extracts a fossil in the Gobi desert, one of many exciting discoveries he has described in scientific magazines.

You can't visit the Dinosaur Age, but thanks to computerized animation, documentaries and feature films, the distant past can seem amazingly real.

 Walking With Dinosaurs (BBC)

 IMAX 3D cinema, Science Museum, Exhibition Road, South Kensington, London, SW7 2DD, UK

 www.dinosaurlive.com and www.dinosaurs3dmovie.com

Books and magazines

If you are fascinated by dinosaurs and other prehistoric animals, it's hard to beat illustrated reference books. Many magazines contain up-to-the-minute news about dinosaur discoveries.

 The Kingfisher Dinosaur Encyclopedia by Michael Benton (Kingfisher)

 Visit your local library to discover a whole range of dinosaur books.

 www.nationalgeographic.co.uk